LIAM BORRETT

Liam Borrett trained at the Drama Centre, London. His work as a writer/director includes *Dancing* (Etcetera Theatre); *Hannah* (Miniaturist Festival, Arcola Theatre); *This is Living* (Bedlam Theatre, Edinburgh Festival Fringe 2014). As a director his work includes *Boileroom* (Miniaturist Festival, Arcola Theatre).

T0347054

Liam Borrett

THIS IS LIVING

NICK HERN BOOKS

London

www.nickhernbooks.co.uk

A Nick Hern Book

This is Living first published in Great Britain in 2016 as a paperback original by Nick Hern Books Limited, The Glasshouse, 49a Goldhawk Road, London W12 8QP

This is Living copyright © 2016 Liam Borrett

Liam Borrett has asserted his moral right to be identified as the author of this work

Cover image: Rekha Garton

Designed and typeset by Nick Hern Books, London
Printed in Great Britain by Mimeo Ltd, Huntingdon, Cambridgeshire PE29 6XX

A CIP catalogue record for this book is available from the British Library

ISBN   978 1 84842 584 2

Woodland
CARBON
www.woodlandcarbon.co.uk
NICK HERN BOOKS
Printed on Carbon Captured paper

This is Living received its London premiere at Trafalgar Studios 2 on 17 May 2016, with the following cast:

ALICE	Tamla Kari
MICHAEL	Michael Socha

Director	Liam Borrett
Designer	Sarah Beaton
Lighting Designer	Jackie Shemesh
Sound Designers	Daffyd Gough
	Sean Gallacher

Producer	PW Productions
General Manager	Will Bourdillon
Production Manager	Amie Shilan
Company Stage Manager	Roshan Conn

Marketing Filming	Potion Mixtures Productions
Marketing Photography	Rekha Garton
Marketing Graphic Design	Flavia Fraser-Cannon at Blue Pie Media
Marketing Campaign	EMG
PR	Chloe Nelkin Associates

An earlier version of the play was performed at the Bedlam Theatre, Edinburgh Festival Fringe in August 2014.

Author's Note

Thank you to the many people who have contributed and helped shaped the play since its initial conception in 2012, including the pool of actors who have read and performed Alice and Michael, and the company of the 2014 Edinburgh Festival try-out. Thank you to family and friends for their support, and to Peter Wilson and all at PW Productions for their invaluable, continual support and dedication.

L.B.

For Mum and Dad

Characters

ALICE, *twenty-two to twenty-eight*
MICHAEL, *twenty-five to thirty-two*

Note on Text

The play is intended to be performed with minimalist set, the changes in time and location being indicated by light and sound.

(*) Indicates a change in time/place.

(…) Indicates that a sentence trails off.

(–) Indicates that a sentence or thought is cut off.

This text went to press before the end of rehearsals and so may differ slightly from the play as performed.

ACT ONE

Monday 4th July. Just after midnight; Sunday, minutes ago.
A riverbank. Otley, West Yorkshire. The water laps by the bank,
the wind slips through the nettles. MICHAEL (*thirty-one*) *still*
in yesterday's clothes, sits, staring down at the bottom of the
bank. The body of ALICE (*twenty-eight*) *lays face-down at the*
edge of the water.

He stares at it, for too long a time.

He moves towards her, crouches down. Her clothes and hair are
soaked, her shoes missing, her face and neck spattered with
mud. He gently lifts her face out of the water, stares into her
eyes, distant, lifeless. Beat. He lifts her body up onto the bank.
Looks at her face, one final moment before closing her eyes.
Proceeds to make his way back up the hill.

Without warning, ALICE *lurches up to sitting as water explodes*
from her mouth. She collapses back down to the ground, her
eyes snapping open.

He stares at her, unable to comprehend the situation, as she
rolls over and pushes herself up onto her hands and knees,
laughing uncontrollably.

ALICE   Have I been on the Blue Nun?
Fucking, Echo Falls?
Told ya before, jump me when I start heading
towards the Echo Falls…

She pushes herself up to standing, her balance
somewhat lacking.

She notices that she's soaked.

Rained?
Would have been nice of ya to –

She laughs. He just stares at her.

Fuck did we get out here?
Like Blackpool all over again, lucky I didn't start
on the red.

MICHAEL   Fuck off –

ALICE   We got Berocca? Shop still open? What is it,
like, eleven?

She with Mum?
She'll kick my arse, you wait, blaming you for
this, telling you that now.

Beat.

MICHAEL   Fuck off –

ALICE   Fancy us? Huh? Fancy us? Fucking, soggy biscuit –
Get a kiss?

She goes to kiss him. He steps back. Looks at her.

MICHAEL   Should stop.

ALICE   We're not having any more, no.

MICHAEL   You're –

ALICE   What you been on, Desperados?

MICHAEL   Fuck off…

ALICE   Ey, this is us now, imagine if we did this all
the time, you wonder how people do it –

MICHAEL   Come on, mate.

ALICE   Going down fucking, Co-op, middle of the day –

She laughs.

MICHAEL   Come on, ya fucker.

ALICE   Take me back will ya, walking seems to be a bit of
an issue.

MICHAEL   On with ya –

ALICE   Need some sleep.

MICHAEL   Am asleep –

ALICE   Alright, Broadmoor, half a litre of tequila down you an' all by the sounds of it.

MICHAEL   On the settee –

ALICE   Christ, how much have you had?

            He looks at her. Begins to laugh. Gets down on his hands and knees.

MICHAEL   What ya doing this for, ya daft twat –

            He starts slapping his face.

            Not the time for this –

ALICE   What ya doing?

MICHAEL   Gotta get up, mate –

ALICE   Acting the mental –

            The slapping gets harder and harder.

            You're gonna hurt yourself –

MICHAEL   Gotta be going –

ALICE   Mike –

MICHAEL   Get up.

ALICE   Stop it –

MICHAEL   Please –

ALICE   Stop!

            He stops.

            Fucking hell, boy –

            This is why we don't drink! I'd be running through the streets singing fucking, Vengaboys if you hadn't found me.

            Come on, should sleep it off.

MICHAEL   Am asleep –

ALICE   You can keep saying it as much as you like, still don't make any sense.

MICHAEL   I'm on the settee –

ALICE   Why would you be on the settee?

MICHAEL   Can't do this –

ALICE   Do what?

MICHAEL   Not yet –

ALICE   Alright…

Alright then. You're asleep. Snoring ya head off. Where am I then? Fucking Narnia?

He reaches out. Touches her face, palpable, solid. She laughs.

You alright?

MICHAEL   Do you not –

ALICE   Not –

MICHAEL   What, nothing?

ALICE   You've lost me –

MICHAEL   What do you remember?

ALICE   Remember?

MICHAEL   Yesterday –

ALICE   What about –

MICHAEL   Yesterday –

ALICE   I dunno –

MICHAEL   What do you mean you don't know?

ALICE   Means I don't know, I don't –

MICHAEL   What do you remember?

ALICE   Can hardly fucking stand up –
Told ya, shouldn't have let me drink.

MICHAEL   You haven't been drinking.

ALICE   Then why do I feel like there's a train in me head?

MICHAEL   What. Do. You. Remember?

ALICE   I. Don't. Know.

MICHAEL   On the bus, yeah?

ALICE   Yeah –

MICHAEL   I needed to –

ALICE   You were, yeah, you were finding somewhere to –

MICHAEL   You were gonna take her down here –

ALICE   I did.

            I did, we were here, she was –
            In me lap –

MICHAEL   Right, come on, think –

ALICE   What ya doing?

            What's this?

            What ya doing?

MICHAEL   I'm –

ALICE   You're scaring me.

MICHAEL   I need you to –

            Sorry –

ALICE   It's alright, it's –

MICHAEL   Please –

ALICE   Mike –

MICHAEL   Just –

ALICE   We were –

            Beat.

            We –

MICHAEL   What –

            *She changes colour instantly as her heart begins
            smashing against her ribcage.*

            *Her stomach heaves up into her mouth, she
            swallows. Her legs barely hold her weight.*

ALICE   Where is she?

MICHAEL   Up the hospital.

ALICE   What, near roundabout?
           One near roundabout?

MICHAEL   Think it is –

ALICE   Who's with her?

MICHAEL   Your mum's up there.

ALICE   What does she look like?

MICHAEL   They're keeping her in, she looks better than she
           did, but they're gonna –

ALICE   Can you drive? You alright to drive?
           Fuck do that matter, come on –

MICHAEL   Wait –

ALICE   Come on –

MICHAEL   What do you mean?

ALICE   Need to see her, need to –

MICHAEL   You can't, can you.

ALICE   Why not?

MICHAEL   I'm trying to tell ya –

ALICE   Give me the keys.

MICHAEL   Listen a minute –

ALICE   Give me the keys, we're wasting time.

MICHAEL   Listen to what I'm saying to you.

ALICE   I'll listen in the car.

MICHAEL   You're not hearing me.

ALICE   Gotta get up there, gotta get her home,
           get her better, all her things around her,
           get her her Disney –

MICHAEL   You can't go to the hospital.

ALICE   It's not the time for this –

MICHAEL   You wouldn't wake up…

            This hits her.

            She takes in the information momentarily, before
            throwing the impossibility away.

ALICE   I'm not gonna tell you again, you're starting to
            upset me now, our little girl, our daughter, is laying
            in hospital, with fuck knows what wrong with her,
            and you're standing here telling me this bollocks.

MICHAEL   You weren't moving. Your hair was soaked.
            We saw you.

ALICE   Saw me? What are you on about?

MICHAEL   You were laying here. You weren't –

ALICE   Well it can't have been me, can it, come on –

MICHAEL   It were you.

ALICE   You're wrong.

MICHAEL   I'm not.

            Beat.

ALICE   Me.
            This is me. This, here, now.

            I'm sorry, but you're wrong –

            Whatever's happened, whatever you think
            you've seen –

            It's alright. I'm here. I'm here. Alright?

            Misunderstanding. Doesn't matter. All sorted.

            Her. Gotta get her better. Come on…

            She takes his hand. He winces, lets go of her.

MICHAEL   You're cold.

ALICE   What?

MICHAEL   You're freezing –

ALICE   We're in a field, it's midnight,
            we're in the middle of a field, it's cold –

            He offers his hands to her.

MICHAEL   I'm not cold.

ALICE   So?

MICHAEL   You're cold, your skin is cold.

ALICE   So I'm cold!

            I'm also here, listening to you speak, I can hear
            you and you can hear me. I can feel the air going
            into me mouth, into me chest, I can feel this grass,
            right, it is wet, it is damp, I can feel me legs, me
            hands, look –

            *She takes his hand, presses his fingers to her
            carotid pulse. He stares at her. She drops his hand.
            Feels it herself. Nothing. She shakes it off, checks
            her wrist. Nothing there, either. She checks his, it
            beats fast.*

MICHAEL   I'm not wrong.

ALICE   You are.

MICHAEL   I'm not.

ALICE   You have to be –

            You –

            What the fuck –

            Beat.

            Look, I'm all up for, fuck it, everyone has their
            beliefs, believe what you want, don't mind, don't
            want it at my door, but give or take, if that's what
            you like, that's what you like…
            But listen to yourself.
            Listen to what you're saying.
            It can't happen…

            I'd be in the ground,
            I'd be rotting in the ground and I'm not, I am here
            with you.

Now for the last time, will you give me the bloody
keys please…

MICHAEL   Couldn't get through to ya. Kept going to –
Tried a couple of times, just nothing –

I come through there, and I just see this man and
this, this man and a woman, and they're holding
her, and I haven't got a clue, can't see you,
don't know where the hell you are –

I go over, sorta turns into a bit of a run, the closer
I get –
I get here, and you're still – Can't see you.

She's all wet, soaked, absolutely, drenched,
He gives her to me, and he just, jumps in,
fucking, hero, dives in, he's gone for so, fucking –
Comes up, couple of minutes later, got you
with him, your face comes up first.

You look –

The strength on him, Christ –
Pushes you up like you were –
she starts pushing on your, blowing in your mouth,
he gets his phone, and she's just screaming,
shaking her head all over the place,
I'm trying to hold her but she won't stop.

Do you know how long they take to get here?
Do you know how long?

Guess –

Twenty-two minutes.
Twenty-two minutes it takes –
And I think – That's a long time.

And when they do get here, they can't do anything.
Nothing they can do, apparently –

Except they say, all they say, they both say it,
man and a young girl, she comes over,
and she says, yano, 'Really sorry,' no she says –
'I am ever so sorry about this.'

'I am. Ever so. Sorry. About this.'

Beat.

Your face –

You looked so shocked.

They take us back, get the key halfway in the door, swing it open and they all turn, all of them – Stephen, Grace, your mum and your dad, all, staring – and they all know, instantly – Your mum starts crying –

ALICE   Stop.
         Please.

         Beat.

         Don't know what this is, big wind-up, whatever, maybe it's not planned out the way you thought it would, maybe you think you're in too deep, don't care, I'll forgive you, but tell me you're just taking the piss –

MICHAEL I'm not joking.

ALICE   Please.

MICHAEL I'm sorry –

                              *

London. A Tube carriage, Piccadilly line towards Cockfosters, December 2010.

ALICE (*twenty-two*) *tries to keep her footing in the crowded carriage,* MICHAEL (*twenty-five*) *barges into her.*

MICHAEL So sorry!
         Fucking hell, can't swing a cat in here, can ya –

         She doesn't respond.

         How ya doing, you alright?

         Ya good?

ALICE   Yep.

           Beat.

           You?

MICHAEL   I'm good, yeah –

ALICE   Right then –

MICHAEL   Where you getting off?

ALICE   Shouldn't really be telling you that –

MICHAEL   It's alright, I'm not a rapist.

           Beat.

           She laughs.

ALICE   Arsenal…

MICHAEL   Arsenal, nice one.
           Go Hammers!

ALICE   That's West Ham –

MICHAEL   Nah –

ALICE   No, really –

MICHAEL   Sure?

ALICE   Live there, so –

MICHAEL   Just checking, see if you were –

ALICE   You don't follow football do you –

MICHAEL   Just wanted to talk to you.
           Don't normally do things like this –

ALICE   Things like what?

MICHAEL   Talk to people.

ALICE   Don't normally talk to people?

MICHAEL   Oh, no I mean I talk to people –
           Not a mime. Not miming things all day –
           Not in a box…

           He mimes being in a box. She laughs.

*

An hour later. MICHAEL *has woken.* ALICE *stands in the middle of the meadow, alone.*

*

MICHAEL   Got everything ready for Crimbo?

                 ALICE *looks a bit bemused but eases into conversation.*

ALICE   Sort of, done a bit today,
                 left it a bit last-minute, yano what it's like –

MICHAEL   Got 'em all something nice have ya?
                 Mum, Dad, boyfriend and that –

ALICE   Just vouchers for me mum and dad.

MICHAEL   Boyfriend and that –

ALICE   Oh God no, thank fuck, not this year.
                 First single Christmas in ages.
                 Got rid of that twat months back –

MICHAEL   Sorry to hear that…

ALICE   You on your own as well?

MICHAEL   Yeah, same, yano, lonely –

ALICE   Lonely? I'm not –

MICHAEL   Not lonely, I mean, just, waiting…

ALICE   Waiting for what?

MICHAEL   The right – Michael – Cox, as in the, plural of –

                 She laughs, he offers his hand, she shakes it.

ALICE   Alice –
                 Moon. As in the –

MICHAEL   Moon –

ALICE   The moon, yeah –

MICHAEL   What ya doing now, Alice Moon?

ALICE   Sainsbury's.

MICHAEL   Wanna get some food?

ALICE   I am gonna get some food…

MICHAEL   With me.

ALICE   Now?

MICHAEL   Yeah.

ALICE   Forward –

MICHAEL   Overstepped the mark, sorry –

ALICE   Do this with a lot of girls?

MICHAEL   It's a first, if I'm honest with ya, not normally this spontaneous.

It's taken me twelve stops to ask you this –
Should have got off at Cally Road, fuck knows
where I am now. But that's alright, that's okay,
I got to speak to you today.

ALICE   This food –

MICHAEL   Don't worry about it –

ALICE   What, like a date?

MICHAEL   Look at me, fucking moron –

ALICE   Go on then –

MICHAEL   You what?

ALICE   You get me wankered though and I'll fucking
have ya –
Got things to do tomorrow, gotta go see my sister.
She's just had a baby.

Carrie. They've called her Carrie –

MICHAEL   Ah nice one, you two the same age then or?

ALICE   Sort of, year older than me.

MICHAEL   Why, how old are you?

ALICE   Twenty-two, how old are you?

MICHAEL   You tell me, what d'ya reckon?

ALICE   I dunno, thirty?

MICHAEL   Fucking hell, do I look thirty?

ALICE   Twenty-seven?

MICHAEL   Less offensive, keep going –

ALICE   Twenty-six, twenty-five –

MICHAEL   Bingo, twenty-five–

ALICE   Christ, get him a bus pass!
           Twenty-five… Taking a twenty-two-year-old out
           for a drink –
           You wanna be put on the fucking list, mate…

MICHAEL   The what?

ALICE   The list – kiddie-fiddler…

MICHAEL   I'm not a –

ALICE   Oh, no, I'm not saying you are –
           Well, I mean, you might be –

           'Each to their own'…

           Beat.

           Sorry.

                              *

Three hours later. ALICE *stares at the river. Tries to fight her tears. Manages. Barely.*

                              *

MICHAEL *stands in their living-room doorway, car keys in hand.*

He stares around the silent room.

                              *

ALICE *runs to the bank's edge and attempts to throws up over the side. Nothing comes. She tries, again and again, still nothing. She falls onto her back, exhausted. She pushes herself up to standing, tries to centre herself, attempts to dance.*

*

The Winchester, Angel, 1 a.m. The music swells, ALICE *up at the front, lost in it.* MICHAEL *watches her dance. She notices him watching her, beckons him over. He reluctantly joins her, begins to sway. She encourages him. Bit by bit, his confidence grows. He grins.*

*

Her room. Two hours later. Moonlight pours in through the curtains. They're off their faces.

ALICE   When was standing this fucking hard?
            Do you want coffee, or tea, doesn't have to be
            coffee – Think Dad's got a bottle of Jameson's
            tucked away –

MICHAEL   Probably shouldn't have any more...

ALICE   Cracking food!

MICHAEL   Twenty quid for spag bol!

ALICE   Should have gone up 'Spoons!
            Love a good 'Spoons.

MICHAEL   Burger. Beer –

ALICE   Been here though?
            Fucking two quid dearer than anywhere else.

MICHAEL   Right... Rip-off... Merchants...

ALICE   So expensive.
            Fucking Twix is like, sixty-nine pee, what's that
            all about?

MICHAEL   Mental –

ALICE   And where are the trees?

            Not saying we were like the fucking
            Eden Project back home, but yano,
            didn't think you'd have to drive
            half an hour just to go and bloody look at one.

            How long you been here?

MICHAEL   I dunno, year? Ever since –

ALICE   Warmed to it yet?

MICHAEL   It's alright –

ALICE   It's a shithole.

MICHAEL   Think you'll end up staying?

ALICE   Just think London's for when you're young.

Doesn't feel like home yet.
Don't know if it ever will.

Wouldn't wanna die here –
Christ, half the people here haven't ever seen a
bloody cow.

*

The injustice and confusion of it all overwhelms her.

She screams.

*

She starts to laugh.

MICHAEL   What?

ALICE   Do you not think it's funny?

MICHAEL   What is?

ALICE   This.

This point.

Only time we don't know anything about each
other yet.

Won't be able to do this again –

MICHAEL   No.

ALICE   I for one find that really exciting.

Beat.

I like dancing.

MICHAEL   What?

ALICE   Dancing. Calms me down.

             At school, if someone were pissing me off,
             they'd always let me go into the cupboard at the
             back of the room and dance. Not like, a whole
             routine, just enough, then I'd come back in when
             I was calm.

             There was this girl, in me class, all the way up
             until sixth form –
             Liberty Abbot.

             Which if you think about it is a really fucking
             stupid name.

             Liberty. Abbot.

             And it seemed that her whole purpose, her whole
             fucking reason for breathing, was to make me feel
             like shit on a daily basis.

MICHAEL   She sounds nice –

ALICE   The girl was a cunt!

             And not being funny right, hardly white as snow
             herself.

             The worst tan I have ever seen in me entire life.
             Looked like a fucking settee.

             No word of a lie, if you'd put a throw round her
             shoulders someone would have fucking sat on her.

             He laughs.

MICHAEL   You're funny.

ALICE   I thank you.

MICHAEL   You have lovely hair.

ALICE   I thank you again.

MICHAEL   How'd you get hair like this?

ALICE   Dunno, genetics?

MICHAEL   It's beautiful.

ALICE   Dad's got the same, looks shit on a bloke.

MICHAEL   Like fire, that is –
             You're like, this, beautiful, fire –

             She blushes. Gets herself flustered.

ALICE   God, are you sure you don't wanna drink or
             something? Such a bad –

MICHAEL   You're brilliant –

ALICE   Haven't even taken me coat off –

             She struggles to get her arms out of her coat.

             I just wanna say, I don't do this with everyone.
             Bring them home and that, day I meet them.
             There's not like, a huge stack of them in the
             wardrobe or nothing –

             They laugh.

             Shh! Me dad gets up in an hour –

MICHAEL   Early –

ALICE   I know! Fuck that for a packet of Quavers –

MICHAEL   Well, gotta take work where you can get it.

ALICE   Where'd yours work?

MICHAEL   They –

ALICE   Are they retired?

MICHAEL   No, no they're not retired.

ALICE   I'm gonna smoke, do you want one?

MICHAEL   Nah, you're alright, cheers –

ALICE   Don't smoke?

MICHAEL   I don't, no.

ALICE   Is it alright, do you want me to go out the window?

MICHAEL   Nah, you're alright, one's not gonna hurt me.

             *She grabs tobacco and papers from her coat
             pocket, begins to roll.*

ALICE   Don't tell Mum and Dad, they don't know.
             I'll do a cheeky bit of Febreze-ing later.
             Should stop.
             Had them patches, don't do fuck-all –

             Might go to the health centre.
             They do these pills right, apparently,
             makes you feel sick when you smell them,
             don't really know what's in them though.

MICHAEL   When did you start?

ALICE   I dunno, like, twelve, thirteen…
             Know I shouldn't, just need an incentive.
             When I have kids,
             I'd stop then, just, yano? Like that, just stop.

             Wait, what, ever?

MICHAEL   Nah, my um, my mum and dad –
             They both – You know? So I just –

             She rams the tobacco back into her coat pocket.

ALICE   I'm sorry –

MICHAEL   You're alright, long time ago.

ALICE   When?
             God, going on about jobs, fucking hell,
             Alice Moon.
             Sorry, I do this –

MICHAEL   It's alright, you weren't to know.

ALICE   Opened a right can of worms.
             You don't have to talk about it, we'll just –

MICHAEL   No, no it's okay.
             He went right after I was born, never knew him,
             found out he had it just before Mum found out she
             was having me.
             Held on though, long enough to see me.
             Loved his fishing, she said. Mad about –

             And then Mum was just last year – Nineteenth
             of April.

It's funny really, he'd smoked all his life, right from when he was little, but Mum… She'd never even touched one. Always thought that were funny.

ALICE   What was her name?

MICHAEL   Lily.
           – Lily and Michael.

ALICE   What was she like?

           MICHAEL *stares at her, doesn't know where to start. Weakly smiles, shakes his head.*

           It's alright, it's okay, it's hard, I mean I've not really got anything that I can compare it with, but I imagine it's really –

           Go on, ask me something else, let's change it up a bit –

MICHAEL   Like what?

ALICE   Anything, come on. What'dya wanna know?

MICHAEL   Do you work or anything? Got a job?

ALICE   I do, yeah. Er, it's not a big, don't laugh at me, I work in a café – And I know that sounds really stupid, and, I'm dead shit at it, you know what I mean? Like, dropping, fucking, plates on the floor, swearing at people, but, money's money, int it – My dancing, I love, but that's not really practical, yano? I'd like to teach it, to er, kids and that, but again, I don't know if that's something I would be able to do, full time. Bit optimistic. Yeah, I dunno, what about you? What do you wanna do, what do you wanna be?

MICHAEL   I wanna be a dad.

ALICE   You what?

MICHAEL   Sorry –

ALICE   No, no, not like in a –
           Most people just don't say that, yano what I mean?

That's really honest, that's lovely that is, why, why's that, why's that the thing?

MICHAEL   I dunno, I just, yano, I had, I was really lucky, I suppose, with Mum, and, yeah, I just, for a little while now, I thought, yeah, I'd like to be able to, to be that person yano? Just to, look after them. Just yeah, just really wanna have children.

ALICE   You can have mine –

Beat.

I am full of it tonight, it's the wine. It's the wine, this is – I'm telling you now, right, I'm not a pisshead or anything, but you gotta warn me, you see me heading towards that Echo Falls, you gotta, put a fucking straitjacket on me, tie me to a chair –

I – I think that's lovely, I think that's really, wonderful.

MICHAEL   You?

ALICE   Yeah, I would.
Yeah.
I think I'd be a bit shit, but, you'd just muddle through, wouldn't ya –

It's been a lovely night, hasn't it.

MICHAEL   It's been great.

ALICE   What was she like?
Your mum –

Was she nice?
I bet she were lovely, bet she were a star-keeper, that one.

He stares at her. Takes a deep breath. Wonders where to start.

MICHAEL   We argued a lot.

He laughs.

I think we liked to argue.

And I like to think I fought pretty hard some
times, but, she'd always get ya, somehow –

To the point. Yano?

Wouldn't cross her.
Heart of gold, but you wouldn't wanna –

'You cross me once, I'll let it slide,
but like fuck are you doing it a second time.'

Like to think I've got that.
I dunno, I think I'm a little more, gullible maybe.

Beat.

She didn't make a fuss or anything.
All the way through.
Sitting in the doctor's, going home in the car,
she just –

She just took it.

And I think she wanted to cry, think she wanted
to scream, but just thought, what good would that
do, for everyone else?

That's the sort of person she was.

It got really bad.

Couldn't walk.
Couldn't go to the toilet.
Couldn't take a bath.

And there's me.

Your bloody, child, giving you a bath.
And she'd just take it –

I don't think I could do that –

Beat.

Fucking loved her.
I hope she knew that.

Sometimes I think, I hope she knew that.

Beat.

Still talk to her –

That mental?

Sometimes I think she's listening.
If I'm feeling down. If I'm feeling like shit.

Say 'Hiya Mum, how are you? Y'alright?
How's it going on up there?'

Sorry, I'm fucking rambling on –

ALICE   You looked after her?

MICHAEL   Yeah.

Yeah.

Got really aggressive.
Unsalvageable, laid up in bed best part of three
months before –

And she didn't moan once.
High as a kite, no fucking clue what she were
saying –
But she didn't moan once.

That's my mum.

He starts to cry. Laughs.

Bet you're glad you asked that!

Christ, fucking, bundle of attractiveness.

Yano what?

I feel a bit of a twat,
and I know I shouldn't, nothing on your part,
you've been lovely, I just don't normally –

I've gone right embarrassed.

ALICE   It's okay, it's sad –

MICHAEL   Yeah. Yeah it is.

I should –

Before I make more of a twat of myself I suppose –

Thank you, for tonight, you're right, has been
a lovely night, wouldn't have changed it for the
world, and if you wanna, if you wanna meet up
again, don't have to, don't feel obliged, but if
you wanna, that'd be –

Okay –

*He stands, goes to leave. She grabs hold of his
waist, turns him around. He stares at her, unsure
of what happens next. She takes his hand, presses
it to her heart. Takes her index and forefingers of
her other hand, places them on his carotid pulse
to complete the circuit. Beat. They break, giggling.
She kisses him.*

*

Monday 4th July. 11 p.m. MICHAEL *stands at the foot of his
bed, listening to his voicemail. He mouths along with the
recording, word-perfect.*

ALICE   (*To* MICHAEL.) Alright lad?

Did ya find somewhere?

(*To Lily.*) Babe –

(*To* MICHAEL.) Just wondering where you are
and that –

(*To Lily.*) Darlin' –

Beat.

(*To* MICHAEL.) We're, just, chillin, aren't we,
just –

(*To Lily.*) Yeah –

(*To* MICHAEL.) Should have just gone in nettles,
who in their right mind's gonna wanna look at that?

Better be worth it, better have had Andrex
double-quilted –

Beat.

We're down bottom.

She's seen the swans, so, you've got time.

Give us a ring when you're –

Beat.

We'll seeya in a bit.

To listen to the message again, press three.
To delete the message, press hash.

*

An hour later. MICHAEL *finds himself in the meadow again.*

ALICE   Where ya been?

MICHAEL   I've –

ALICE   Three days I've been standing here –

MICHAEL   What?

ALICE   Three days –

MICHAEL   It's Monday.

ALICE   What?

MICHAEL   It's Monday.

ALICE   I've –

MICHAEL   I saw you yesterday.

ALICE   No.

MICHAEL   Just yesterday –

ALICE   Feels –

            You sure?

            Monday?

MICHAEL   It's Monday.

            Beat.

ALICE   How is she?

MICHAEL   She's –

ALICE   She breathing better?

MICHAEL   Yeah.

ALICE   Been up there today?

MICHAEL   All day.

             Left this afternoon.

ALICE   Did ya go home?

MICHAEL   All went back earlier –

ALICE   And she were –

MICHAEL   She were fine.

ALICE   Yeah –

                              *

November 2011. A B&B in Truro. MICHAEL *(twenty-six)*
paces. ALICE *(twenty-three)* *lays across the bed.*

MICHAEL   Small you said, small gathering.
             Largest small gathering I've ever been to –

ALICE   I know a lot of people…

MICHAEL   I know a lot of people,
             and I never expected them all to be standing in
             your mother's living room.

             Beat.

             Thought Stephen had forgotten the ring.

             See his face?
             Blind panic, that –
             Never seen a man change colour so fast.
             Same colour as his suit –

             Thought I were gonna have a bloody heart attack,
             daft twat –

ALICE   That's the thing isn't it, that's what the whole
             day's about –
             Big build-up, rising and rising and then suddenly,
             at the, climax,
             there's that, release –

*

ALICE   And what, she's sleeping?

MICHAEL   Sorry, give me a –

ALICE   No, sure.

            Sorry –

MICHAEL   It's just been –

ALICE   Sorry.

MICHAEL   It's –

ALICE   Come here –

            She goes to hold him. He moves away.

MICHAEL   I'm –

ALICE   Okay –

            Beat.

            You eating?

            Did you eat today?
            Still stuff in the fridge?

MICHAEL   I don't know.

ALICE   See if Mum'll –

            Fuck.

MICHAEL   They're both –

ALICE   Please.

            Beat.

            But they're alright?

MICHAEL   Gonna go stay with them.

ALICE   Yeah.

MICHAEL   Probably go tomorrow.

ALICE   That's good.

MICHAEL   Just thought –

ALICE   No, it's good.
Shouldn't be alone.

MICHAEL   No one's crying –

ALICE   What?

MICHAEL   None of them.

ALICE   Okay –

MICHAEL   That weird to you? Weird to me –

ALICE   What, even Mum?

MICHAEL   Everyone, just nothing –

ALICE   Guess it's different for different people, int it –

MICHAEL   I can't fucking stop –

ALICE   Well that's no surprise, ya never could –

Beat.

It's the shock, int it –

They'll –

MICHAEL   Cos I want to, yano?

I would actually like to talk it through,
deconstruct it a bit, make a plan, actually do
something, and I can't –

ALICE   Yeah, but it's still –

MICHAEL   Cos if I'm honest, I've got fuck-all idea what
I'm doing –

ALICE   Love, stop a minute –

MICHAEL   What?

ALICE   Not everyone's like that –

MICHAEL   I know that –

ALICE   Sure that's what you really wanna be doing?

MICHAEL   What else can I do?

ALICE   You're allowed –

MICHAEL   What?

What am I allowed?

*

MICHAEL   Did ya try your mum's lemon drizzle?

How many did she put in it? Fucking hell –
Half a bloody Jif factory in there,
thought it were gonna have Maureen's face off –

ALICE   Like a bit of, drizzle, ey?

MICHAEL   It were nice, zesty –

He paces around the outside of the bed.

ALICE   Love, sit down a minute –

MICHAEL   Can't, got a lot of energy, yano?

ALICE   Good, that's good –

MICHAEL   Gotta move, gotta do something –

ALICE   Liking the sound of it –

MICHAEL   You alright?

ALICE   Me?

MICHAEL   You look –

ALICE   I'm, yeah, cracking.

MICHAEL   What do you wanna do?

ALICE   Can think of a few things –

MICHAEL   What ya got in mind?

ALICE   I'll do you a bloody mime in a minute –

MICHAEL   It's nice this room, int it –

ALICE   Top.

MICHAEL   How you'd imagine it and that, dead nice –

ALICE   Sets the mood –

MICHAEL   All petals –

ALICE   Looked good –

MICHAEL   Better on telly though, don't you think?

           Smashing on the telly,
           in real life, fairly inconvenient,
           scraping bits of foliage off your duvet –

ALICE   Will you come here –

MICHAEL   Sure you're alright?

ALICE   I'm good to go, mate.

MICHAEL   Mate?

ALICE   You are my mate –

           Am I your mate?

MICHAEL   Yeah.

ALICE   Right, then –

           Wanna make a child?

           Beat.

MICHAEL   With –

ALICE   Ideally.

                              *

A long pause.

ALICE   Did ya wanna talk about it?

MICHAEL   I would, yeah –

ALICE   Okay then –

MICHAEL   Not with –

           Beat.

ALICE   Okay.

MICHAEL   I didn't –

ALICE   No. Understood.

MICHAEL   Just –

ALICE   It's alright, I get it, I get ya –

MICHAEL   That's not –

ALICE   It's okay.

MICHAEL   It's not okay.

ALICE   They're there, I'm –

Fuck knows –

MICHAEL   What do I do?

Beat.

ALICE   I don't know.

MICHAEL   Right –

ALICE   I'm sorry –
I'm not gonna lie to ya, I don't know what you
should do. But I know that they're gonna be more
than willing to help you with her –

MICHAEL   Oh no, they have been. Picking up all the pieces.
Which, if you think about it, is a really good job –
Because frankly, two days in, I've already managed
to surprise myself with how little I actually know,
you would have thought I'd have picked more up.

ALICE   Well that's me, that is –

MICHAEL   How'd you work that one out?

ALICE   Doing it all for ya –

MICHAEL   Well I clearly weren't paying much attention,
was I –

ALICE   You were, working, providing –

MICHAEL   But where it really counts –

ALICE   It'll get easier.

MICHAEL   Like turning up halfway through.

ALICE   Think I knew how to do any of this in the
           beginning?

MICHAEL   It's too late –

ALICE   What do you mean?

MICHAEL   It doesn't work, it's like I'm trying to hold water –

ALICE   Michael –

           Beat.

MICHAEL   Sorry –

ALICE   No, no it's –

MICHAEL   What did you do today?

ALICE   I sat here.

           Beat.

MICHAEL   Look, I should be getting off –

ALICE   You don't have to –

MICHAEL   See how she's doing –

ALICE   We should –

MICHAEL   Maybe you should get some sleep.

ALICE   I can't –

MICHAEL   Could try –

ALICE   Have tried –

           Beat.

MICHAEL   I should –

ALICE   Right.

MICHAEL   I'll catch you tomorrow –

ALICE   Yeah.

MICHAEL   You alright?

ALICE   Yep.

MICHAEL   Yeah?

ALICE   Yep.

            Beat.

MICHAEL   Sure?

ALICE   Yes.

            He leaves. She looks down at her right hand.
            It shakes involuntarily. She flexes her fingers,
            the communication between brain and hand not
            instantaneous. She tries again and again. The
            shaking subsides momentarily before returning
            again.

                              *

Kerry Matthew's wedding reception. March 2012. Music pulses.
ALICE *(twenty-four) and* MICHAEL *(twenty-seven) fight to be*
heard over the sound system.

MICHAEL   I've asked for it!

ALICE   What?

MICHAEL   Asked him to play it!

ALICE   I can't hear ya!

MICHAEL   Been over to the man –

ALICE   Can't hear ya!

            Did ya have the beef?

MICHAEL   Said he'd stick it on in a bit!

ALICE   Bit of beef, did it taste alright to you?

 MICHAEL   When are they gonna do the cake?

ALICE   You feeling alright? I'm feeling a bit –

            Bit concerned!

MICHAEL   Think it's chocolate or Madeira?

ALICE   Need some air –

MICHAEL   What?

ALICE   Air.

MICHAEL   Can't hear what you're saying!

ALICE   Air – In, out, in, out.
            Air!

MICHAEL   I can't –

ALICE   I'm going outside –
            Outside –

            He shakes his head.

            Back in a minute!

                              *

*Tuesday 5th July. Midnight. The two of them sit side by side.
A long pause.*

ALICE   How was today?

MICHAEL   –

ALICE   What did you do?

            Go out?

MICHAEL   –

ALICE   So what, you stayed in?

MICHAEL   Yeah.

ALICE   Did you eat?

MICHAEL   Bits –

ALICE   What did you have?

MICHAEL   Just –

ALICE   Are you gonna go out? Not, like, not in a, but –

            Beat.

            How's Mum?

            Silence.

Just gotta keep her talking, yano?
Even if it's just, nonsense, just talk at her, just so
she, feels part of a conversation, that'd be a really
good thing to –

And her? She sleeping?

Silence. He nods, barely.

What did she look like?

MICHAEL   What?

ALICE   Before you came here, what did she look like?

MICHAEL   Just –

ALICE   Take her long?

MICHAEL   Four hours.

ALICE   Just her routine, it's been –
           I'd got it down to half an hour –
           Did she look peaceful?

MICHAEL   Normal.

ALICE   Normal?

MICHAEL   Just looked –

ALICE   Okay –

                            *

MICHAEL *finds* ALICE *in the car park. She's rubbing her
stomach.*

MICHAEL   You alright?

ALICE   Yeah, yeah, just feel a bit –

MICHAEL   What? You alright?

ALICE   Yeah, just a bit. Yano?
           Just feeling a bit funny.

MICHAEL   You okay? Do you want me to get you –

ALICE   No, it's fine, it'll pass, really, it's fine.
           Don't have to worry –

MICHAEL   Okay.
           Coming back in?

ALICE   Yeah, just wanna have a little bit of a sit-down,
           haven't had a sit-down, can't remember the last
           time I sat down –
           Hours –

           It's a lot easier when you're about fourteen, could
           do it then. A lot harder than it looks, doing the
           Macarena with child.

MICHAEL   I'm surprised you remembered all the moves –

ALICE   I'm surprised I remembered all the moves…
           Total recall, that.
           Dead proud of myself.

MICHAEL   Gonna be alright?

ALICE   Yeah, yeah, just have a little breather, little
           catch-up –
           I'll be right in, do Saturday night –

           I'll be alright.

                            *

ALICE   Can I say something?

MICHAEL   –

ALICE   Been thinking –

MICHAEL   –

ALICE   Maybe we should start making some sort of plan –

           For when –

MICHAEL   We had plans –

           Beat.

ALICE   Yeah.

           Yeah, we did.

MICHAEL   What do I do with them?

           Beat. She doesn't know.

ALICE   Just while we've got the opportunity, yano?
           While we're able –
           Just if there's anything you wanna know, maybe
           we should get it all out.

           And I know that's asking for the world, but it
           seems sensible. Seems practical.

MICHAEL   Can we not just sit here?

ALICE   Sit here?

MICHAEL   Just us. Just be here.

ALICE   There's things to consider –

MICHAEL   Escape a little –

ALICE   Escape?

MICHAEL   Me and you.

ALICE   It's not about –

                              *

MICHAEL   They'll be doing that cake soon.

ALICE   Guess –

MICHAEL   Think it'll have marzipan?

ALICE   Yeah, usually, don't they –

MICHAEL   You can have mine.

ALICE   Thanks, mate –

           Her stomach twinges again.

MICHAEL   Is it the –

ALICE   No, no, we're good –
           Christ, how much bloody energy do you use
           doing this?
           They got Lucozade in there?
           Need a whole bloody vat of it –

MICHAEL   Looked lovely, didn't she –

ALICE   Oh God, couldn't believe it, well I could, bloody
           beautiful –

           Went to school with her, went to playgroup
           with her.
           We're old. I'm old. Be drawing my pension soon.

MICHAEL   Did you cry?

ALICE   I did, did cry –
           There she was, coming down the, and I just went –

MICHAEL   I cried.

ALICE   Bet ya did, ya little pussy.

MICHAEL   Not as much as ours –

ALICE   Well no, that's not humanly possible, is it –

MICHAEL   I was proud.

ALICE   Thought you had a fucking tsunami coming out
           ya face –

MICHAEL   I was happy!

ALICE   Thought Noah were gonna have to build another
           Ark –

                              *

ALICE   We're irrelevant –

           Beat.

           What?

           Have been for three years, we're irrelevant, babe.

           More silence.

           I'm not blind. I know you're –

           And that's what I'm saying –

           I just want you to feel prepared.

           Beat.

           Mike –

           Please –

I'd really appreciate it if you were just, not a full
conversation, I understand that's –

But if you could just –

Beat.

Okay.

Okay.

*

MICHAEL   Won't be able to do this for much longer –

ALICE   It's a child, not a wasting disease –

MICHAEL   Whole going-out and that –

ALICE   Fuck that mate, down Tiger Tiger every night, me –

Her stomach twinges again.

MICHAEL   Should sit down –

ALICE   It's that pissing beef, forty quid a head she spent
on that, we'll all be going home with salmonella –

It's this one, blame them for the short temper.

MICHAEL   Been pregnant two years?

*

ALICE   Have you talked to her about it?

MICHAEL   –

ALICE   Mike –

MICHAEL   No, no I haven't.

ALICE   I know you're gonna wanna wait for the right,
time, but –

MICHAEL   But –

ALICE   I don't know if there's ever gonna be one –

MICHAEL   She's three.

ALICE   I know that.

MICHAEL   What do I say to her, then?

          Go on –

          Tell me, what do I say?

          Sit her down, look her in the face, and she'll start
          doing that smile thing, like she doesn't really
          know if we're being serious or not, and whilst
          she's doing that, I tell her, what –

          Her mum's, what –

          Beat.

          I need to go.

ALICE   Yeah. Maybe you should.

MICHAEL   Check her –

ALICE   Yeah.

          Beat.

          Yeah.

          Beat.

MICHAEL   Gonna be alright?

ALICE   I'll be fine.

          *Her right hand starts to tremble. She tries to hide
          it from him, turns away.*

MICHAEL   What's that?

ALICE   Nothing –

          I dunno, it's nothing.

MICHAEL   Right.

ALICE   Go see how she is.

MICHAEL   Do you want me to stay a bit?

ALICE.   No.

          Beat.

          Look, I'm only trying to help –

She turns back. He's already left. She looks down at her right hand. It trembles uncontrollably again. She flexes it. Without warning, she loses consciousness, falls forward, regaining consciousness just seconds before hitting the floor. She catches herself with her hands. Holds herself steady. Pushes herself back up to standing

*

MICHAEL   Certainly getting bigger.
            If that's the politically correct phrasing of that
            sentence –

ALICE   Gonna fucking lamp you one in a minute.

            Only time I can be a total lard-arse and no one can
            say a fucking word.

MICHAEL   Excited?

ALICE   Yeah.

            Beat.

            Yeah.

MICHAEL   Big year.

ALICE   When will we sleep!

            She laughs.

            Worth it.

            Beat.

            Could do with a fucking fag –

MICHAEL   You've done really well.

ALICE   Do you not think we can lure someone out here?

            Someone's gotta need one at some point –
            Just the smell, if they can just stand there, we'll
            be away.

MICHAEL   You'll be fine, just need air.

ALICE   Yeah.

MICHAEL   Do you want a drink?

ALICE   Yeah, could do.

MICHAEL   Coke?

ALICE   Wine.

MICHAEL   No.

ALICE   Jäger.

MICHAEL   No.

ALICE   Ketamine.

MICHAEL   No.

ALICE   One night of passion and suddenly everything becomes illegal –

MICHAEL   Coke?

ALICE   Yes, Dad.

MICHAEL   Good.

ALICE   Good.

He leaves.

ALICE *rubs her stomach, trying to stem the pain.*

Suddenly, from inside her, a massive twinge.

She bends double, her insides churning.

Another violent, extended pull.

She begins to panic.

She reaches up under her dress, inside her underwear.

Her fear is confirmed.

She pulls out her hand.

Thick, dark, blood.

She stands, staring down at her fingers.

MICHAEL *returns with the Coke.*

She looks up from her hand, their eyes meet.

Blackout.

End of Act One.

ACT TWO

March 2012. Two hours after we left them in the car park.
ALICE *sits on the edge of the hospital bed.* MICHAEL *stands
beside her, leaning against the cubicle wall. She stares down at
the wad of tissue she has been handed, slowly resigns herself to
the practicality of the act, begins to wipe away the blood stuck
to her hands and the inside of her legs.* MICHAEL *quietly
drops down to her eye level. She won't look at him.*

*

Their living room. About an hour later.

MICHAEL   Do you want a hot-water bottle?

ALICE   I'm alright.

MICHAEL   I'll put the heating on.

          Beat.

ALICE   Quiet –

MICHAEL   It's three in the morning –

ALICE   Where are the foxes?

MICHAEL   Probably asleep.

ALICE   Put some music on.

MICHAEL   What?

ALICE   It's too quiet.

MICHAEL   Don't know if it's the right time –

ALICE   Why?

          Cos of them? Her next door?
          Deserves to be fucking woken, stupid cow.

MICHAEL   Al –

ALICE   What?

You've never liked her, don't go getting all high and mighty now.

MICHAEL   Maybe in the morning –

ALICE   Is the morning. Sun's up.

MICHAEL   Do you want tea?

ALICE   Should ring Kez –

Reckon they're there yet?
When did they leave? Just after us?

MICHAEL   They didn't go.

ALICE   What do you mean they didn't go?

MICHAEL   Think they wanted to make sure we were alright.

ALICE   We're fine, it's over with.

Can't change anything.
Get on with it.

MICHAEL   Do you wanna talk about it?

Not right now maybe, but when you're ready
I think it might be worth having a chat.

ALICE   What is there to talk about?

Beat.

We had something, now we don't –

I bought a lottery ticket last week, and when I got home, it had fallen out of my pocket. I had something, it could have been something more, but then it wasn't there any more.

MICHAEL   Al –

ALICE   I'm going to bed.

*

Wednesday 6th July. 9 p.m. MICHAEL *sits in the living room, staring at the wall. Moves to the record player, turns it on. 'Guava Jelly' by Johnny Nash. He sits listening, lost in it. Turns the volume up, louder, louder, the room shaking. Lily begins to cry upstairs. The music pulses.* MICHAEL *throws his head back towards the ceiling, screams into the darkness.*

*

Three hours later. MICHAEL *stands in the meadow with his back to* ALICE. *Her legs tremble. She tries to remain balanced. Her arms shake. She tries to hide this from him. A long silence.*

ALICE   Did you open them?

MICHAEL   None of them.

ALICE   You gonna?

MICHAEL   Don't think so.

                    Why would you send someone that?

ALICE   Show they care –

MICHAEL   Oh, right. Okay.

ALICE   Get someone else to do it, share the load a bit –

MICHAEL   I'd bloody love a bit of, share the load, yeah –

ALICE   Stephen –

MICHAEL   Yeah, he's alright, that one, always underestimated him to a certain degree but you know what, top lad, out of all of them, he's really stepped up –

ALICE   Well, I imagine they're –

MICHAEL   What?

ALICE   I imagine they're hurting –

MICHAEL   We're all hurting –

ALICE   I've told ya, talk to her –

MICHAEL   You're right. Could do, couldn't I –

                    Yano what I did this morning? Looked at her, sitting in the kitchen, I looked at her across the

table and you know what I felt? I felt a little bit
ashamed.

Next Wednesday by the way. Date for the diary –

ALICE   What?

MICHAEL   We've gone for Wednesday.

ALICE   That a bit soon?

MICHAEL   Best we could get at short notice –

ALICE   Do you have to book?

MICHAEL   A lot of people die –

ALICE   Alright, I've never –

MICHAEL   What did ya wanna wear?

ALICE   What?

MICHAEL   What do ya wanna wear?

*

July 2012. Their living room.

MICHAEL   It's six –

ALICE   I know.

MICHAEL   Had to use Christmas paper, didn't have any –
            It's alright, she won't know the difference...
            Said we'd be there about quarter to,
            so we might wanna get a move on soon.

ALICE   Sorry, what?

MICHAEL   Said we might wanna get going soon, it's nearly
            time –

*

ALICE   We should –

MICHAEL   No.

ALICE   Wait –

MICHAEL   No –

ALICE   If you'd just let me say what I wanna say –

MICHAEL   Why?

ALICE   What do you mean, why?

MICHAEL   Raking it all up, digging it about, what good's that
             gonna do?

ALICE   Thought it might help –

MICHAEL   Help?

ALICE   Might be useful –

MICHAEL   How can that be useful?

ALICE   Help ya to start looking at it –

MICHAEL   And what if I don't wanna look at it?

ALICE   You don't even know what –

MICHAEL   What if I have no intention of looking at it?

ALICE   Don't be –

MICHAEL   Don't be what? Go on –

ALICE   Like that –

MICHAEL   Like what?

ALICE   You're not serious –

MICHAEL   Am I not?

ALICE   What, ever?

MICHAEL   I don't know –

ALICE   And how's that gonna work?
             Gonna sit like this till the end of time?

MICHAEL   Feels like it, at the moment, yeah –

             What?

ALICE   Sorry?

MICHAEL   What –

ALICE *What –*

    Fantastic –

MICHAEL What now?

ALICE You –

    How can you be that selfish?

MICHAEL You what?

ALICE Gone deaf?

    That's –

    No, seriously, that's fucking reassuring int it, really settling, that –

    There was a little bit of me thinking, yano what?

    Despite this, fucking, car crash, actually, she might be alright, might possibly get through this, cos he's so fucking solid, and now what, you're telling me what, that's not gonna happen, throw that all away, piss that up the wall –

    Yeah?

    Right okay, don't worry about it then, mate –

    You keep doing that –

    Her right hand trembles, she shakes it off.

    For fuck's sake!

          *

ALICE I don't think I can go.

MICHAEL Go?

ALICE Tonight.
    I don't think I can…

MICHAEL Okay…
    It's just we said we would.

ALICE I know.

MICHAEL   You'll be missed –

ALICE   We're only gonna have to come straight back.

MICHAEL   What if we just go for a little while?
Hour or so, give her her present,
sing her 'Happy Birthday' –

ALICE   Michael –

MICHAEL   It's her birthday, love. Please –

ALICE   My back's disgusting. Fucking hate this heat.

MICHAEL   Well they're doing it in the back garden, so –

ALICE   I'm not going.

He goes quiet.

If you've got something to say –

MICHAEL   It's nothing.

ALICE   It's not nothing.

MICHAEL   I think, it's a little harsh, if I'm honest with ya.

ALICE   Well thanks for your honesty –

MICHAEL   Alright, I'll go by myself.
But I think it's a shame.

Beat.

Look I get it.
I know where this is coming from –

ALICE   Do you –

MICHAEL   Course I do…

ALICE   You haven't got a bloody clue.

MICHAEL   Don't you fucking dare.

Sorry –

ALICE   No, go on. Go on then –

Silence.

Oh you know what, I'm not fucking doing this now.

MICHAEL   No, come on, why not now?
             Been tiptoeing around this for months.

ALICE   Why is it this hot? Door open?

MICHAEL   Yes.

ALICE   Fucking sauna –

MICHAEL   Why are you changing the subject?

ALICE   Because I don't have the energy, alright?

             Go, you'll be late.

MICHAEL   I'm not going without ya.

ALICE   You'll cope.

MICHAEL   No, I won't cope.

ALICE   This isn't the time.

                              *

MICHAEL   Want it to stop.

             Beat.

ALICE   What?

MICHAEL   –

ALICE   What ya saying?

MICHAEL   –

ALICE   Stop it –

MICHAEL   Why? Been thinking it all week, best all round –

ALICE   What, for her? Mum and Dad?

MICHAEL   All of them, look at me, hanging about, mard-arse,
             ghost at the fucking banquet, what use is that? Just
             end it all, stop it there –

ALICE   Don't you dare –

MICHAEL   Why?
             I don't want it, I don't want any of it, without you
             in it I don't want it.

ALICE   Do you know how lucky you are? To stand where
           you're standing?

           What, just gonna leave her? Let everyone else
           pick it all up, all they've done for you? You
           wanted to be a fucking dad, mate, come on, step
           up to the fucking plate, be a dad, yano what I'm
           talking about? Now's the time to shine, time to
           prove yourself and what are you doing?

           Fucking coward –

MICHAEL   Lucky? Ever sat with your family and decided on
           the day you're gonna put your wife in a box? Call
           that lucky?

ALICE   Yeah and whose fault is that?
           I'm not fucking stupid alright, I get it, we're all
           here because of me.
           And the moment I attempt to try and rectify that,
           look what I get –

           'What do you wanna wear?' Fucking hell –

           She stumbles, holds her balance.

MICHAEL   Who the fuck are you?

ALICE   Yano what? I don't know. I do not know any more.

MICHAEL   You used to be –

ALICE   She's gone. She's going in the ground next
           Wednesday, she's fucking vanished, mate.

MICHAEL   Well, I'd love to see her again –

ALICE   Got it so bad, haven't ya –

MICHAEL   We're going through exactly the same thing.
           Cut me a bit of slack, yano what I mean?

ALICE   Yeah.

           Yeah.

           Exactly the same. Fucking photocopy.

           Here –

*She takes his hand. Presses it to the bottom of
her throat.*

There?

That –

Got that?

Beat.

I will never –
Hitting my legs when she wants something.
Laughing, at things that aren't even funny.

All that –

That there? That accurate?

She moves the hand down to her stomach.

Sat there going on a year. Now look at her –
Carries *me* now. Don't know she's doing it, does
she, but look at her –

Got that an' all?

He falls silent.

I can go on –

He pulls his hand away.

Nah, here's the best bit.

*She grabs his hand again, moves it to her ribcage,
roughly between her lungs, where her heart used
to beat.*

That's gone. That's empty. Some fucker's gone
and taken that out –

Beat.

Never know normal, will she.
Three fifteen, everyone else, home with Mum,
not her.

To say sorry to her, get on my knees, for that girl –
Mumble, out an idea, of an apology.

She laughs.

Mum –
Bit inapplicable now, int it –

Beat.

She's not coming, calling back down them stairs,
fifteen, sixteen, things start getting a bit weird, bit
new, she's not –

I do get it though. I do –
It is hard. Fucking brutal, mate –

But you know what?
That's just what it is.

No one does give you a clap at the end of the day.

You get to bedtime, she hasn't fallen down the
stairs, swallowed a knife, and I'd say then you've
just about earned the right to close your eyes for
half an hour and think about yourself.

And you know what?

I don't feel like crying either.

They might not, and I definitely don't –

What'd be the point?

Beat.

So what do I do?

Fucking, useless. Dripping all over the place –

Tell me. What do I do?

Thought I'd try and help –

Try and do something –

Cos let's face it, you've been –
Haven't ya –
Putting yourself aside. Holding me up.

Done alright, haven't ya, you've been –

And I think there's a bit of you that thinks I
haven't noticed that, haven't appreciated that –

But I have.

More than I think you realise.

Beat.

Don't know what's happened though, don't know
where he's gone,
gone somewhere, I dunno –

Left me with you –

You with my mum, my dad, my family.
Laughing, eating, still doing all that –

Just suddenly doesn't seem to be enough any
more –

Which is the bit I'm struggling to get my head
around –

When they've always been enough before –

When you've needed help,
when you've not known what to do,
when I'm standing in the car park,
bleeding into my hands –

And that little girl, who never did anything –

My beauty of a girl.

Whose only fault, was trusting, me.

*Her balance finally goes. She falls down onto
her knees. He goes to help her up, she pulls her
arm away.*

If you won't look at this, for her,
whilst they put everything that's going on inside
them aside to hold a safety net, for you –

Maybe, yeah.

Yeah.

Beat.

You dare waste her, and I swear –

She hits him. Hits him in the legs, then the chest, as high up as she can reach. Again and again. She slips, falls down to her elbows.

She screams at the floor, then up at him. Full-on screams at him, loud, primal, messy. She tries to calm herself down, breathing through her teeth.

Beat.

He turns, leaves. She sinks to the floor as her ribcage collapses, her hands balling, squeezing, violently shuddering.

*

MICHAEL   Fucking hell, Al.
I know this is hard –
But you're hurting me.

Beat.

ALICE   Had it planned –
We were doing alright, weren't we?

We were ready, I think.
For the next bit.

MICHAEL   What are you saying?

ALICE   Did we get too settled?

MICHAEL   I don't understand…

ALICE   Shouldn't have planned it.
Then we wouldn't have been disappointed.

MICHAEL   It'll happen.

ALICE   I don't know if it will.

He sits down next to her. Silence.

MICHAEL   Can't see it?

Beat.

ALICE   It's not there any more.

A long silence.

Christ, say something.

MICHAEL   Give me a minute.

What, nothing at all?

Another long silence.

All that's coming –

ALICE   But if it doesn't?

MICHAEL   It will –

ALICE   But when it doesn't –
What do we do?

MICHAEL   We do like we've always done.

ALICE   And you'd be alright with that?
You'd be content with that?

MICHAEL   What makes you think I wouldn't?

ALICE   First night I met you I said what do you wanna
be and you said, from ya heart, out ya mouth,
I wanna be a dad.

I cannot promise you that.

I wish I could, alright, I wish I had a different body,
one that was capable of so much more than this,
but I don't, this is what I've got.

And I cannot be that source of disappointment.
I won't do it to ya.

MICHAEL   Don't want them instead of you.

ALICE   You say that now, but in five, ten years,
I think you'll notice the difference.

MICHAEL   We're still young –

ALICE   But we won't be.
We'll be at the right point.

MICHAEL   Just think it's about, staying positive, yano?

ALICE   I wish I could –

Wish I could.

A long silence.

MICHAEL   There's three things I like about you –

ALICE   Michael –

MICHAEL   Three things –

          More than that, obviously,
          but these three, I think are important, are, vital –

          One.
          You are incapable of getting halfway through
          a sentence, without starting another, I think you do
          this, because your brain gets miles ahead of ya,
          and you've got so much you wanna get out, it just
          sorta comes out in this big old mess –

          And I like that, I find that so endearing, so honest.

          Two.
          You openly refer to yourself by your full name.
          In third person.

ALICE   I don't.

MICHAEL   Yeah, you do.

          And that's brilliant, that's a wonder. Because
          heaven forbid, if I end up getting Alzheimer's that
          is gonna come in really handy.

          Beat.

          It'll be a girl, won't it. Has to be.
          Be like you, won't she, your light –

          Three.
          That's three. That, light –

          He points at her ribcage.

          Normally there, glowing away.
          Maybe she'll have that. I imagine she will.

          Beat.

          I'm just so certain about this, yano?

          That's the problem –

I've done it. Found my person, don't want
anyone else.

It's been a rough couple of months, I know it has –
But in spite of all that –
This still doesn't seem unachievable to me.

So I'm gonna make you a promise and I'm gonna
stick to it.

If you genuinely think this goes no further,
there's no point to any of it, wanna call it a day –
I won't stop you.

But I'm telling ya.
If there's still something there, ten per cent –
Worth getting up in the morning,
then Christ, I'm willing to wait for it if you are.

*

MICHAEL *sits at the edge of his bed in the dark, staring at the
ceiling. Through his tears, you can just about make out the
following.*

MICHAEL Hiya Mum.

How you getting on? You alright?

Yeah it's been a bit of a shite one really –

You alright then? You and Dad –

Yeah.

Beat.

Need a bit of a favour, don't I.

You know how you've been watching and that,
sort of, seen everything going on and everything,
seen it all haven't ya. Well I hope you have. Hope
you have.

Beat.

She's gone, Mum.

And I don't know what to do –

She's gonna be, probably Wednesday I would
have thought, she's gonna come –

You get to meet her.

Are you excited?
I would be, I'd be – Top of the world.

She's brilliant.

But she's gonna be a bit, she's gonna be a little bit,
yano, it'll be new for her, won't it –

You'll have to show her what to do, what you can
do, all the things, all the people and that, yeah?

You're gonna have a right old time you are.

Beat.

She's good, yeah. I don't think she really
understands, but –

She's beautiful.

She's getting a right little, bossy girl, you know
what I mean? She's like her mum. She's just like
her mum. You'll see it, won't ya – When you meet
her, you'll know what she's like, you'll know
exactly what she's like –

His tears begin to overwhelm him.

Just take care of her, yeah?

Fucking, love her.

Hope everything's alright.
And I'll try me hardest to come and speak to ya,
I'll try and have a little chat next week, let you
know how it goes and that.
Just about ready, her mum and dad, they've been –

Okay, I'm gonna go now, look at me, hey?
Hey? Look at me.

I always cried didn't I, always cried at everything,
everything. You wouldn't think I'd have any left
would ya, hey?

You take care of yourself, and Dad, say hello to
Dad for me.

Love ya, Mum.

Beat.

She'll be there soon.

*

ALICE *lays by the water's edge.*

*She quietly sings the second verse of 'Guava Jelly' by Johnny
Nash under her breath.*

*Her right hand shudders. Her eyes fix on it. Watching. It shakes
again. She scrunches it up into a fist, tries to hold it still. Her
left hand joins the right. She balls this one too. The two fists
rattle in the water beside her.*

*She rolls onto her chest, pushes herself up to sitting, her body
tired, weighty. Crawls over to the side of the bank. Stares at
herself in the water's reflection. The whole top half of her body
begins to shake. Her arms give way. She falls forward onto her
forehead.*

ALICE   Come on, girl.

> *She pushes herself back up to hands and knees,
> tries to keep her balance. The weight of her body
> overwhelms her again, the shaking knocks her
> back down to her elbows. She looks at her face in
> the reflection, her skin spattered with dirt.*
>
> *Using her right arm to support her, she scrapes
> her hair back away from her face with her left
> hand, holds it up behind her, half-up, half-down,
> before letting it drop back down again. Stares into
> her eyes. With great effort she slowly lowers her
> face down into the water. She holds it under for
> several seconds before lifting it out. She wipes the
> dirt away from her face. She looks down at the
> reflection again. Still not clean. She dips her face
> in again, before pulling it out. Looks. Repeats.*

Again. And again. Still there. She slaps her reflection. Screams.

Beat.

Stares down at the water, then up at the sky. Slowly lowers her head under again. Takes her right hand, forces the head down. She stays there for a long time, but nothing happens. She cannot pass out.

She comes back up, drops onto her back. With the little energy she has left in her legs, she pushes herself back away from the bank's edge. Lays there. Staring up into the blackness. Her gaze is caught by her legs. They have begun to tremble. She glares at them. Subtly, but quickly building, her chest begins to vibrate, then her arms again, then her head, faster and faster, uncomfortable, violent. She tries working against them, tries to keep them still but with little effect. The shaking crescendos, her whole body writhing about in the water.

Just end it!

Fucking stop!

The shaking builds and builds.

Then, a moment. A quiet, little suspension, her whole body held momentarily, before collapsing back down to the ground. She gasps for what little breath she can reach.

Beat.

Nearly breaks. She catches herself, clasps her hands over her face. Holds them there tight. Slowly drops them away from her face. Carefully debates her next move. Looks down at her feet, quivering in the water.

It's time.

She slowly places her hands together. Stares up at the sky. Closes her eyes.

Please.

Her hands shake. She interlocks her fingers,
clenching them tight. It's no good. They won't
stop. She laughs at the sight of them. Looks up at
the sky. Laughs at that too. Then breaks into tears.
She clasps her palms over her eyes again. But it
doesn't work. Her tears seep through her fingers.
She lays there, hands over her face, shivering in
the water.

MICHAEL appears, finds her on the floor. He
picks her up, holds her as she shakes. She wipes
her tears away. A long silence.

Been thinking –

MICHAEL   Yeah?

ALICE   Yeah –

Thought we might, might wanna go out, for like,
a meal and that.

MICHAEL   Yeah?

ALICE   Yeah.

Go down er, go down Bella.

MICHAEL   Bit of Bella?

ALICE   Bit of Bella.

MICHAEL   No where –

ALICE   What?

MICHAEL   Bit more –

ALICE   More than Bella?
Are ya mad?

MICHAEL   Just thinking, we haven't been out for a while,
not formal, we should –

ALICE   Are ya real?

MICHAEL   Yeah –

ALICE   You'd betray Bella?
           I can't go anywhere else other than, I like her,
           she always, satisfies me, to an extent.
           She's like 'Spoons, I wouldn't, 'Spoons, I like,
           yano, I like it simple.

MICHAEL   I've never liked a girl who doesn't like 'Spoons.

ALICE   Exactly. Exactly. So. We should, when this is all –

MICHAEL   Yeah –

           Yeah.

ALICE   What did ya do today?

MICHAEL   Erm, I went out.

ALICE   Yeah?

MICHAEL   Yeah. Went down Tesco.

ALICE   Oh yeah?
           Was it packed?

MICHAEL   It was. It was a little bit full.

ALICE   Basket or trolley?

MICHAEL   Had to get a trolley, didn't have a pound,
           so that was a bit, troublesome –

ALICE   Did you borrow one?

MICHAEL   Had to get cash out then I had to go and buy a
           Twix, so it was a bit of a palaver before I could
           even start, took a little while to get going, but we
           got there –

ALICE   Take her with ya?

MICHAEL   Yeah, she was in the, thing, sat in the thing, so that
           was alright in the end.

ALICE   What did ya buy?

MICHAEL   Just –

ALICE   Fridge running out?

MICHAEL   Yeah, that was the thing, there was a bit of, and I
           don't like to, I don't like to filch, off ya dad, so I
           just thought I'd go out and buy some stuff, so that
           were fun, that were interesting, do you know how
           expensive, Coco Pops have got? I just bought their
           own, Everyday Value, cos I just thought, right,
           they taste the same, don't they, they taste exactly
           the same, so what's the point in that? Why would
           you buy it? You're basically just paying for a
           picture of a monkey, monkey with a baseball cap,
           looking like he enjoys some cereal.

ALICE   Probably doesn't, probably hates it –

MICHAEL   He is lying to himself. And in that lie, charging
           another sixty-five pee,
           so, fuck him.

           What did ya do today?

ALICE   I just –

           Do you wanna drink? Shall we have a drink? We
           should have a drink, I don't have much in – I've got
           water, it is, of the river variety, it may not be,
           greatly hygienic, we can't, I've not got a Britta, but
           maybe, we can, yano, we can get you something.
           What do ya want? G&T, voddy and coke?

MICHAEL   Don't really know –

ALICE   We'll get you something.

MICHAEL   Maybe we shouldn't start drinking, start fighting
           again –

ALICE   Shouldn't –

MICHAEL   No you're right, we shouldn't, lost my voice last
           time –

ALICE   Did ya?

MICHAEL   Well I thought I did, then I realised I was just
           asleep, so, non-applicable, int it, you do start
           wondering what is actually real –

ALICE   It's all real, mate, it's all – non-fictional.

Silence. She stares at him. Beat.

Weren't watching –

I weren't watching her.

She were there, and I'm –

She points away from the bank.

I'm there.

Getting her bread –

She's seen the swans, wants to feed them –
Course she does –

Beat.

And I know what you're thinking. It's crossed my
mind once or twice –

Couldn't ya have done both, Alice?
Couldn't you have afforded our daughter a basic
level of care, whilst you were doing that?

And the thing is, right. Thing is –

I could've, couldn't I?
I could have done that.

But I clearly think, in that moment, that that's too
much of a hassle.

Cos she'll still be there, won't she.
Next to that large body of water.

Three-year-old, perfect balance, perfect
coordination, what's there to worry about?

And it takes me about thirty seconds to realise
what it is that I've done.
And then I think, what the hell are you doing, you
stupid twat.

What, are you, doing?

*She slaps the water with both hands. Listens to the
sound echoing.*

Tried looking for her –

I tried.

A long silence.

Disappointed ya, haven't I.

Beat.

It's okay –

It's okay.

Disappointed myself, so, it's not come as any
surprise, if I'm honest, the natural progression of
things. I'm surprised you're still here, I'd have, I
dunno, maybe I'd have, thought you'd have
fucked off by now.

I don't expect you to stay,
if you wanna leave you can, that's understa–
It's expected, if anything, it is anticipated.

MICHAEL   Why would I go?

ALICE   Why would you stay?

Look at what I've left ya with –

MICHAEL   It's an accident.

ALICE   It's not an accident.

Dropping a plate's an accident, fucking, spilling
ya pint's an accident, how's that an accident?

MICHAEL   She's safe –

ALICE   Well no thanks to me!

MICHAEL   Alice –

ALICE   Please –

I just, I just don't think you should do it to yourself,
and I know you're like that, I know you're
inherently kind, and there will be a bit of you, of
course there will, more than a bit, that just thinks,
you should be like that, and that's brilliant, and in

any other situation, I think that would be fantastic,
so honourable, but I just think, this time, you have
to look at it and think, do I actually feel like that,
and if I'm just doing it to be nice, to be kind, then
I just wouldn't.

MICHAEL   I don't blame you.

ALICE   I bet you don't –

I bet you don't.
But I blame me, and if I'm honest – I don't think I
get past that. I don't think that runs away, so what
does that do to me and you?

Beat.

Exactly, you can't –

MICHAEL   It doesn't change anything –

ALICE   It changes *everything*.

Cos that's it int it, that's the thing, this is the
thing that is there forever and it doesn't go away,
we can't change it, it don't get better, it don't
just disappear, it fucking, sticks and is there for
the rest –

So I'm sorry alright. I'm fucking sorry.
I can't even, that doesn't even, begin to, what I –
But in its simplest form, I apologise, for fucking it.

MICHAEL   I forgive you –

ALICE   Stop –

MICHAEL   I forgive you –

ALICE   No. No you don't –
Why are you still here?

MICHAEL   Cos I fucking love ya, ya twat –

ALICE   You need to go. You need to go now.

MICHAEL   I'm not going anywhere.

ALICE   Please.

MICHAEL   I've made my choice.

ALICE   You can't.

MICHAEL   I've just done it –

           A long silence.

ALICE   Fuck.

           Sorry.

MICHAEL   It's okay.

ALICE   Leaving you with this.
           I'm fucking sorry, mate.

           Beat.

           Come here.

MICHAEL   What –

ALICE   Lay with us. Just for a bit.

           He lays down next to her.

           I miss our bed. Fucking hate grass, yano what
           I mean?

MICHAEL   Yeah, I get ya –

ALICE   Do you like it?

MICHAEL   No, not really, not in this context, it's alright
           normally, but it's been a fucking –

ALICE   Yeah. Fucking river, fucking night,
           I just wanna see the sun, fucking night-time.

           Beat.

           Been a shit week, hasn't it.

MICHAEL   Yeah.

ALICE   I fucking died, yano what I mean?
           Won't be doing that again –

MICHAEL   I miss ya.

ALICE   Do ya? Do you miss us?

MICHAEL   I do, yeah.

ALICE   Miss my jokes?

MICHAEL   Could say that.

ALICE   Was she sleeping?

MICHAEL   Yeah.

ALICE   Getting better?

MICHAEL   Yeah. It's less –

ALICE   Does she look –

MICHAEL   She looks beautiful.

ALICE   She is.

Just love watching her sleep. I love watching her chest, her chest going up and – We made that, that's ours, how magic is that?

Yano what I wanted?

I wanted to see her in her uniform, and I know that sounds –
But that's the only –

How lucky are you?

MICHAEL   How we gonna do this without you?

ALICE   I don't know –

I don't know.

But you will, I think, I think you will.

You're not a coward. I've never thought that. I shouldn't have said it, I've never thought it. You're just – You're just a little bit lost. But that'll – Won't it –

Course it will.

Beat.

What you said before, you won't do it, will ya. What you said, you won't –

MICHAEL   Course I won't –

ALICE   But you have thought about it, it's been in your
          head?

MICHAEL   Yeah.

ALICE   Okay.
          Just promise me though, promise me, love –

MICHAEL   Promise.

ALICE   Cos I think, right, at the end of the day –
          At the end of the day, I don't think it would be,
          I don't think it would achieve anything, would it –

MICHAEL   No.

ALICE   It wouldn't, would it.

MICHAEL   I'm sorry I've been a twat.

ALICE   I'd have done the same.

MICHAEL   No, but –

ALICE   Hey –

          Beat.

          You're gonna be brilliant.
          Fuck – Listen to me, with me compliments –

          You're gonna be brilliant, I know it.

MICHAEL   I can't –

ALICE   Yeah, but even if you can't, I can –

MICHAEL   Means a lot –

ALICE   It's alright. You're very welcome –

MICHAEL   We don't have to stop doing this –

ALICE   Yeah, we do.

MICHAEL   I could –

ALICE   Yeah.

Yeah, but I think, I think the thing is, love.
I think the thing is, you'd stop. And that's –

Beat.

Gotta move forward.

*

Their garden. October 2012. ALICE *drags* MICHAEL *out onto the patio.*

ALICE   Will you stop whining for two bloody seconds!

MICHAEL   What, and we couldn't just stay in the kitchen?
             I've not even taken my shoes off –

ALICE   It's a nice night –

MICHAEL   It's freezing.

ALICE   It's mild, it's a mild night.

             She points to the sky.

             Look at that, that looks like that and you wanna
             be in there –
             What is wrong with ya –

             Take your coat off.

MICHAEL   I'm not taking my coat off.

ALICE   Get comfortable.

MICHAEL   Why, what ya planning on doing?

ALICE   Will ya just sit your arse down.

             They sit.

             Listen.

MICHAEL   What?

ALICE   Exactly.

             Alright day?

MICHAEL   Just normal.

ALICE   What did you do?

MICHAEL   What do you mean?

ALICE   I mean what did you do, describe your day –

MICHAEL   Had to have that chat with Carol.

ALICE   I like her.

MICHAEL   She weren't very nice.

ALICE   Kill her. Kill her with bees.

MICHAEL   Went to Boots. Meal deal.

ALICE   Summer fruits?

MICHAEL   Didn't have any, had to have citrus –

ALICE   Fucking Judas –

MICHAEL   Went home, made to stand in the garden –

ALICE   Will you shut your face, you. It's nice.

MICHAEL   July. Nice in July.

            You?

ALICE   What?

MICHAEL   How did you fill your day –

ALICE   Me? Nothing ya wanna hear about –

MICHAEL   No, go on, you've got me intrigued –

ALICE   It were fine, nothing out of the ordinary –

MICHAEL   Well was it good?

ALICE   Yeah. You could say that.

            Are you thirsty, do ya want something?

MICHAEL   We've only just sat down –

ALICE   I can do you some –

MICHAEL   What's up with you?

ALICE   I'm fine, there's nowt wrong with me, fucking
           top, mate –

           Beat.

           I've got something to tell ya, haven't I –

MICHAEL   I bloody knew it, you done the car in again?

ALICE   No! No, it's a good thing!

MICHAEL   What is it?

           She takes out her phone, flicks through her playlist.

ALICE   Ey, I've practised this. Right –

           Practised this.

           Promise –

           *She places the phone down in front of her.
           Presses play.*

           *The music bursts into life, 'Guava Jelly' by
           Johnny Nash.*

           ALICE *starts to mime actions for the first verse.*
           MICHAEL *begins to laugh.*

           She reaches the chorus.

           *The dancing stops as she slowly places her hands
           on her stomach.*

           She grins as he realises.

           *He grabs her and spins her round, pulling her into
           a hug.*

           *The music grows louder and louder as they laugh
           and cheer, dancing around in the dark.*

                           *

Wednesday 13th August, 2016, early morning.

MICHAEL *stands in his bedroom in the dark.*

*He slides open the wardrobe. Their clothes stand, side by side.
He quietly pulls out his suit. He holds it up in front of him, takes
it apart from the hanger, begins to undress.*

He puts on his shirt and trousers. Stands looking at the tie in his hand.

A noise. He turns on the bedside light.

ALICE *lays in the middle of the bed, the duvet soaked. She looks smaller, fragile. Her whole body shakes quietly.*

MICHAEL   Ayup duck.

She opens her mouth to reply. Nothing comes out. He nods.

Okay.

He sits down beside her. Highlights his suit.

What'dya reckon?

She indicates that he looks 'alright'. Grins at him. He laughs back.

Thanks, mate.

Not done yet, mind –

Holds out the tie. Puts it around his neck. She reaches out to tie it, her hand drops down under the weight of itself. She tries again, again it falls.

It's alright.

Had a little tutorial. With your mother.

He ties the tie with some difficulty.

Took her a good hour, nearly broke the woman –

She smiles. Stares at him. He knows what she wants to know. He looks at the open door.

She's just down there.

Snoring her head off.

Dead good.

She begins to cry. He pulls her over into his lap, cradles her.

Hey –

I think it'll be alright, today.

You can't say, can ya –

But, ya can hope for the best.
All ya can do, int it.

He holds her tight.

Shouldn't worry.

She'll be –
Won't she.

Mustn't worry.

Beat.

I'll get her up in a bit.

Beat.

Blackout.